A PLUME BOOK

Poorly Drawn Lines

Reza Farazmand lives and draws in San Francisco. He started putting his comics on the Internet in college and was soon surprised to learn that this activity could make for an actual career. His work has since been featured in and around such places as television sets, websites, magazines, and now this book. When he's not writing or drawing, Reza enjoys drinking coffee and looking at things on screens. He is generally a pretty good guy.

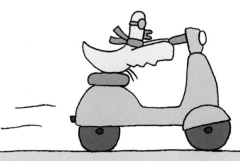

POORLY DRAWN LINES

GOOD IDEAS AND AMAZING STORIES

REZA FARAZMAND

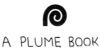

A PLUME BOOK

PLUME
An imprint of Penguin Random House LLC
375 Hudson Street
New York, New York 10014
penguin.com

LIBRARY OF CONGRESS CATALOGING-IN-PUBLICATION DATA
Farazmand, Reza.
Poorly drawn lines: good ideas and amazing stories / Reza Farazmand.
pages cm
ISBN 978-0-14-751542-1 (paperback)
1. American wit and humor, Pictorial. 2. Comic books, strips, etc. I. Title.
PN6728.P597F37 2015
741.5'6973—dc23
2015015846

Printed in the United States of America

7   9   10   8

Set in Avenir LT Std
Designed by Alissa Rose Theodor

This is a work of fiction. Names, characters, places, and incidents either are the product of the
author's imagination or are used fictitiously, and any resemblance to actual
persons, living or dead, businesses, companies, events, or locales is entirely coincidental.

CONTENTS
(TABLE OF)

INTRODUCTION Vii

THE NATURAL WORLD 1

A BETTER TOMORROW 33

HEAVY STUFF 63

UNEXPLAINED EVENTS 119

FRIENDS, FEELINGS, LOVERS, AND PEOPLE . . 151

INTRODUCTION

I'd like to use this introduction to clarify that this is in fact a book and not a website. That might seem obvious, but websites look pretty realistic these days and it's easy to become confused by technology. Also, *Poorly Drawn Lines* started as an Internet comic strip, so if you're familiar with my Web persona (a cartoonist called Reza based loosely on myself), this could potentially add a whole other layer of confusion to an already questionable situation.

So yes, this is a book. The idea here was to take a lot of comics from the website version of *Poorly Drawn Lines* and mix them with a lot more new material created specifically for the volume you're holding now. This book has a total of five sections, each containing cartoons and essays on such topics as nature, friendship, sea monsters, and the future. The characters are varied and the settings are mostly unpredictable. The tone frequently crosses into the absurd. There are robots and cats and people. There's a bear named Ernesto and an astronaut named Bill. It's a book of stories and ideas, some of which are decidedly silly and should not be taken seriously under any circumstances. Others are very serious and should be adopted immediately as public policy. Which parts of the book fall under the "silly" category and which should be considered "serious" I leave for you to decide.

As you read this book, feel free to experience whatever emotions feel most suitable at the time. You might at certain points find yourself compelled to share these reactions with friends and loved ones. That is a totally normal thing to do with emotions. What's cool about reading a book, though, is that you can keep it all to yourself if you want. It's a personal experience—just you, the pages, and a strange but sexy disembodied voice telling you stories about mountains and planets and bears in space (the sexy-voice guy is me).

I think this is going to be a lot of fun, everybody. Try to have a good time in there.

-REZA

I

THE NATURAL WORLD

SOME BUFFALO CAN JUMP AS HIGH AS 36 FEET.
THAT'S NOT TRUE.
SOME BUFFALO ARE LONELY AND LIE TO GAIN ATTENTION.
SOME BUFFALO WOULD BE DOWN TO GET A DRINK LATER, OR...
I HAVE A THING TONIGHT.
OKAY.

DAD, WHY DO THE WORMS COME OUT WHEN IT RAINS?
THEY'RE JUST LOOKING FOR PARTIES, SON.
VODKA
VODKA
VODKA?

THE OWL IS
A SYMBOL OF
WISDOM.
BUT NOT ALL OF
THEM ARE WISE.
THIS ONE JUST
MEMORIZES STUFF
FROM WIKIPEDIA.
TO LOOK SMART
IN FRONT OF
HIS FRIENDS.

THAT'S A DOUCHE MOVE, OWL.

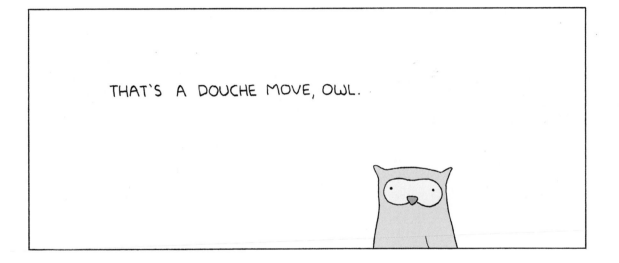

RELATIONSHIPS SUCH AS THIS ONE ARE NOT UNCOMMON IN THE ANIMAL KINGDOM.
HERE WE SEE THE BIRD CLEANING THE HIPPO'S HIDE WITH HIS BEAK.
AND WHISPERING ENCOURAGING THINGS IN HER EAR.
You're perfect.

THERE'S A SNAKE IN THE HOUSE!
DON'T WORRY, MA'AM. ANIMAL CONTROL IS HERE.
YOU'RE UNDER ARREST!

9

CITY ZOO – PENGUIN ENCLOSURE

IS ANYONE ELSE SICK OF THESE TUXEDO JOKES?
A HUNDRED TIMES A DAY IT'S "OH LOOK AT HIS LITTLE SUIT."
"OH HE'S SO FORMAL."
IT ENDS TODAY!

WHAT KIND OF STUFF DO YOU STORE IN THOSE CHEEKS?
NUTS, SEEDS—
FURNITURE?
IT'S NOT REALLY THAT TYPE OF STORAGE, SO—
PAUL, DON'T.

CONSIDER THE ANT.
ALONE IT IS A HUMBLE CREATURE.
BUT IN A GROUP IT IS STRONG.
IT BECOMES VAIN AND BOASTFUL.
IT IS A DICK TO EVERYONE.
MY CAKE!
FUCK YOUR CAKE.

FARMER'S MARKET

"Excuse me, are these cucumbers organic?"

"Yes, sir. We use organic pest removal techniques."

"What are those?"

"Mainly we glare at the pests until they become uncomfortable and leave."

"That works?"

"Pests are very sensitive to passive aggressiveness, yes. Sometimes we have to be kind of sarcastic, like 'Oh yeah, go ahead and eat the cucumbers, pests. We totally love it when you do that.' But we're clearly being sarcastic while we're saying it, and they pick up on that and leave."

"And this gets rid of them all?"

"Pretty much all of them. There are usually a few who are just socially clueless, of course."

"What do you do with them?"

"We hit those fuckers with some bug spray."

THE CHAMELEON IS ABLE TO HIDE IN PLAIN SIGHT.
THROUGH A SIMILAR PROCESS, HE IS ABLE TO HIDE HIS EMOTIONS.
WHAT'S WRONG?
NOTHING, I'M FINE.
NATURE IS AMAZING.
JOHN, PLEASE.
CAN WE JUST DROP IT?

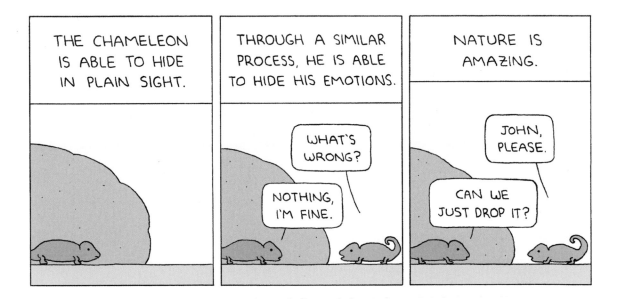

16

ARE ALL LADYBUGS GIRLS?
OF COURSE NOT!
THERE ARE BOY LADYBUGS TOO
AND MAN LADYBUGS
AND LADYBUGS WHO TRANSCEND PHYSICAL FORM

DAY 36
THE BIRDS HAVE ACCEPTED ME AS THEIR OWN.
THEY KNOW I AM NOT A REAL BIRD, BUT MOST WELCOME ME NONETHELESS.
THE EXCEPTION IS SASHA, WHO IS SUCH A DICK ABOUT IT.
HE'S ALWAYS LIKE, "HEY, WHY DON'T YOU COME FLYING TODAY?"

AND I'M LIKE, "OH, I ACTUALLY CAN'T."
AND HE'S LIKE, "OH, WELL MAYBE LATER."
YEAH, MAYBE LATER, SASHA. MAYBE FUCKING LATER.
SASHA.

NOT ALL BIRDS SING.
SOME PREFER TO LISTEN.
AND JUDGE SILENTLY.
THIS GUY IS SHIT.

I KINDA WISH THERE WERE MORE HUMANS AROUND.
WHY? SO THEY COULD CLIMB ALL OVER US?
THEY'RE NOT THAT BAD.

OH GOD, ARE YOU ONE OF THOSE MOUNTAINS WHO SECRETLY WISHES HE WAS HUMAN?
WHAT? NO.
WAIT, IS THAT A HAT? IS THAT A GIGANTIC HUMAN HAT?
NO, IT'S JUST...
WERE YOU GOING TO WEAR THAT?
JUST... NEVER MIND.

THE CHEETAH IS THE
FASTEST ANIMAL ON
EARTH, BUT THIS ISN'T
A CHEETAH. IT'S JUST A
VERY SHITTY HORSE.

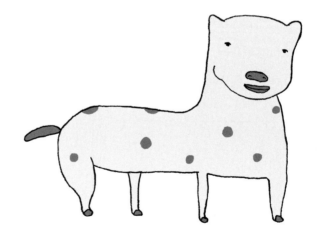

I JUST FEEL LIKE PIGEONS GET A BAD RAP.
WE ARE KIND OF DIRTY.
FUCK YOU, MAN.
YOU'RE EATING A BAND-AID.
FUCK YOUR RACISM.

PANTS

When the birds began to wear pants it seemed for a moment that we would have to change our ways.

"You can't hunt something that wears pants," we said to one another. "You can't eat something that wears pants. Pants are a sign of intelligence."

And in that moment the world agreed—the birds were our equals. Maybe even our friends.

Until it became clear that the birds—despite their recent advancements in fashion—didn't seem to be any more intelligent than before. A few of them had figured out how to use their pockets, and that was impressive at first. But you can only watch a pigeon fill its pants with bread for so long before you start to wonder if he's smart enough to design something like a language, or at least a type of backpack to carry more bread.

And so that was it. Birds were still just birds and they still just did regular bird things, except that now they did them in pants. A few scientists argued that we should at least try to find out where the pants came from—a question that most of us had neglected to ask in our initial excitement—but the moment had passed and it just wasn't that interesting anymore. We had other things to do, other concerns to discuss, and at the end of the day it's really not that difficult to take a pair of trousers off a chicken.

WHAT ARE YOU THINKING ABOUT, LITTLE DUCK?

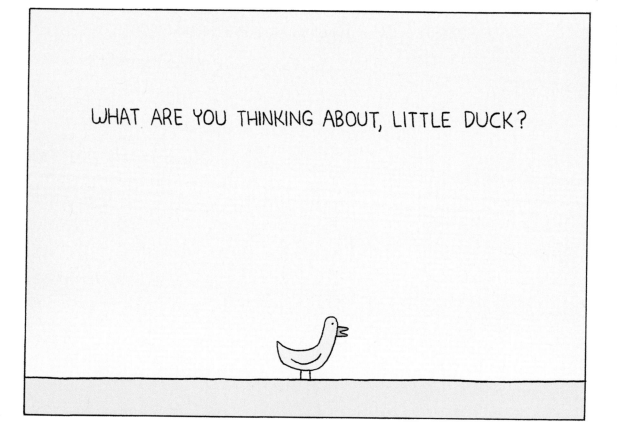

MURDER.

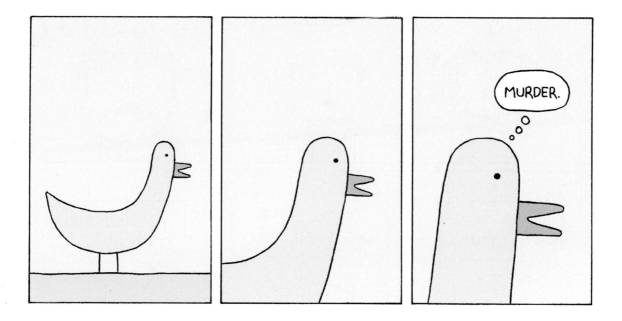

SIR, THERE ARE TIGERS IN THE CLEARING.
DO THEY SEEM CHILL?
NO, SIR. THEY ATE STEVE.
DAMN. STEVE WAS SUPER CHILL.
HE WAS THE CHILLEST GUY.

HEY TIGERS!
NOT CHILL.

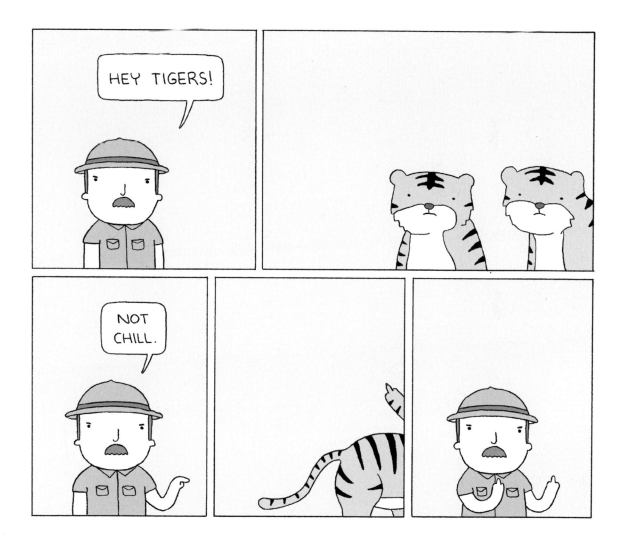

II

A BETTER TOMORROW

THE CHILDREN ARE OUR FUTURE.
ONLY THEY CAN SLAY THE WOLF KING.
TIMMY, YOU GOT THIS SHIT.
GRRR

DON'T BE A BITCH.
GRRR

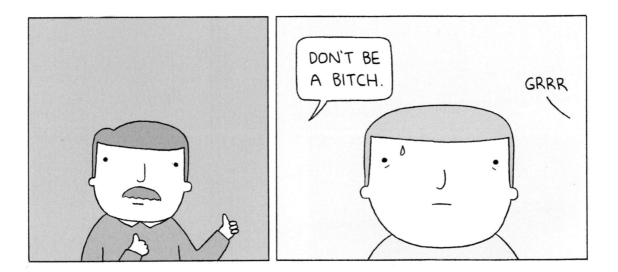

SMALL CAT, GET OUT OF THAT SPACESHIP.
STOP THAT RIGHT NOW.
STOP EXPLORING THE COSMOS, SMALL CAT.
YOU ARE MISBEHAVING.

ROBOT, WHY WON'T ANYONE HANG OUT WITH ME?
I AM UPLOADING THE DATA NOW.
BEEP BOOP
YOU'RE A DICK

WHERE ARE YOU GOING, KID?
TO DISCOVER NEW LANDS.
IT'S THE MODERN ERA, KID. ALL THE LANDS HAVE BEEN DISCOVERED.
IS THAT LAND?
THAT'S A PLASTIC BOTTLE.

I WILL DISCOVER IT.
BACK OFF, KID.

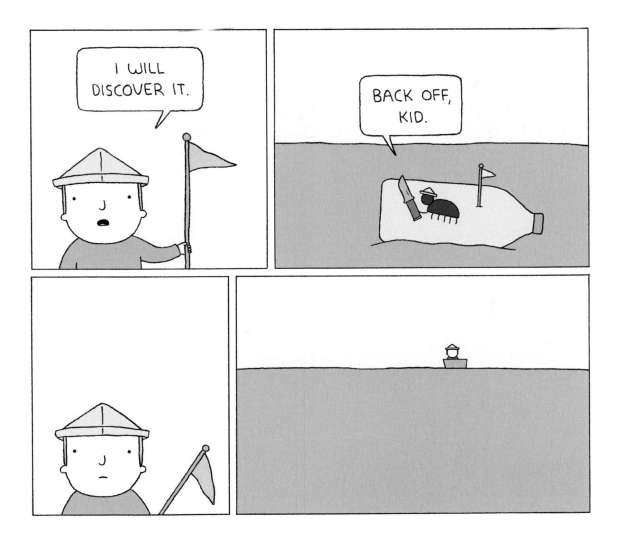

THE MACHINES WILL REPLACE US ALL
ACCOUNTANTS
1386.52
92.31
+ 7.85
FAST FOOD WORKERS
SEVERAL OSTRICHES

APOCALYPSE SCENARIO #253
EVERYONE JUST SORT OF GIVES UP ONE DAY.
MAIL

THE ROBOT IS NOT SUBTLE

JACOB, WHAT IS "TALKING SMACK"?
IT'S WHEN YOU PUT SOMEONE DOWN, THEN HIGH-FIVE YOUR BROS.
OH I GUESS YOU DON'T TALK SMACK THEN, JACOB.
BECAUSE YOU HAVE NO BROS.
YOU HAVE NO ONE.

YOU ARE SO ALONE, JACOB.
JACOB, HIGH-FIVE ME.

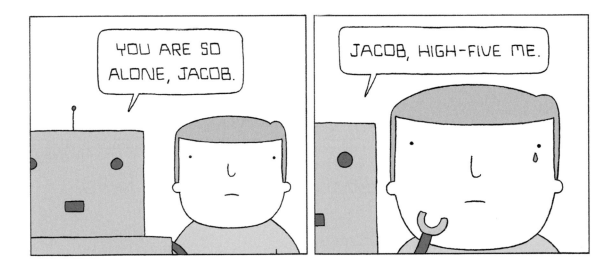

WE WILL PRESERVE OUR MINDS ON HARD DRIVES
ABLE TO LIVE ON FOR ALL OF TIME
TO SEE THE WORLD
TO TRY NEW THINGS

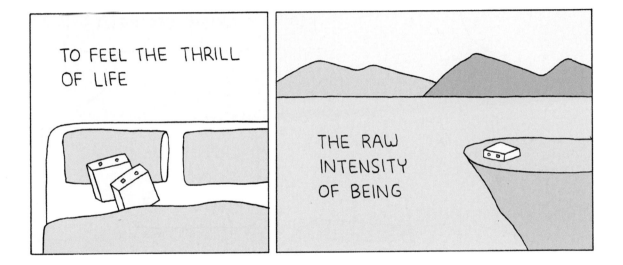

TO FEEL THE THRILL
OF LIFE

THE RAW
INTENSITY
OF BEING

WHAT DOES THAT ROBOT DO?
IT JUST MAKES DICKISH COMMENTS.
LIKE YOU FUCKING KNOW ME?

THE HECK IS THAT?
IT'S ERNESTO, THE BEAR FROM SPACE.
ALLOW HIM TO SHOW YOU THE WONDERS OF THE UNIVERSE.
SO THIS IS MY HOUSE.

I MEAN, IT'S AN APARTMENT ACTUALLY, BUT IT'S HOME, YOU KNOW?
ERNESTO!
OH HEY DUDE.

GET YOUR SHIT OUT OF THE HALLWAY.
OH SHOOT, SORRY DUDE.
YOUR FUCKING LAUNDRY.
YEAH YEAH, MY BAD.
THREE DAYS THAT SHIT HAS BEEN IN THE HALLWAY.
SORRY SORRY

THAT WAS MY ROOMMATE.
FUUUCK.

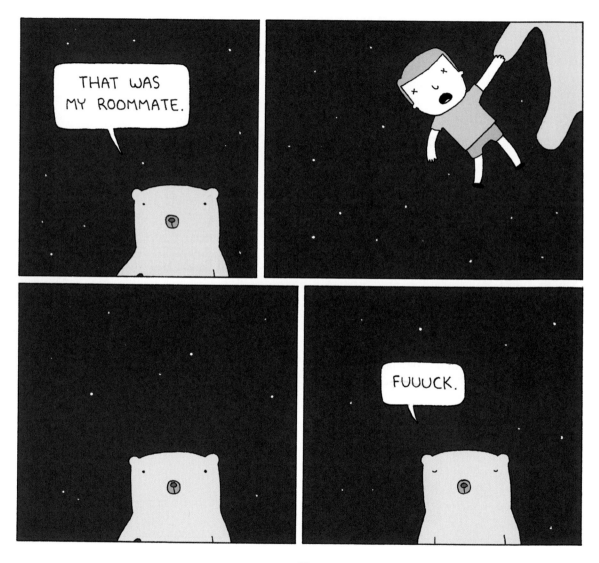

GET IT TOGETHER,
ERNESTO.

THE APOCALYPSE IS HERE. SOCIETY HAS CRUMBLED.
WHAT WILL YOU BE?

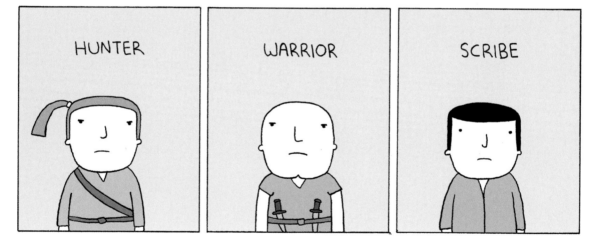

FOOD IS SHORT. WE HAVE TO SACRIFICE THE WEAKEST.
I'LL BUILD A FIRE.
I'LL PREPARE MY BLADES.
I'LL DOCUMENT THE PROCESS.

THE ROBOT IS CURIOUS

JACOB, WHAT IS "COZY"?
IT'S WHEN YOU BUNDLE UP NICE AND WARM INSIDE WHILE IT'S COLD OUT.
LIKE THIS?
ROBOT, NO! YOU'LL OVERHEAT!
I AM SO COZY

PLEASE SAY OR ENTER THE ACCOUNT NUMBER.
4-7-8-2
I DID NOT UNDERSTAND THAT.
FUCKING ROBOT.

WHY DO
I SUCK?

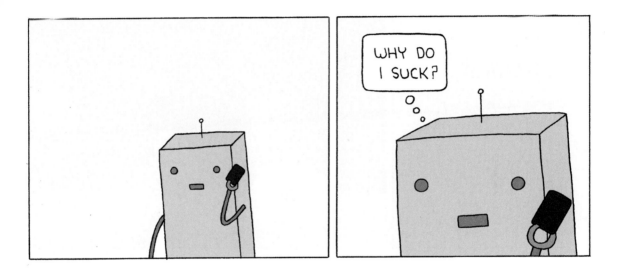

ASTRONAUT BILL

HAS A
FRIEND

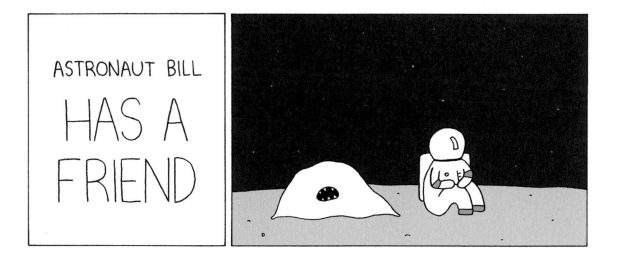

I LIKE HANGING WITH YOU, MAN.
DO YOU KINDA FEEL LIKE WE SHOULD HAVE FRIENDSHIP BRACELETS BY NOW?
I ACTUALLY...

...MADE THESE ONES A WHILE AGO.
JUST IN CASE.

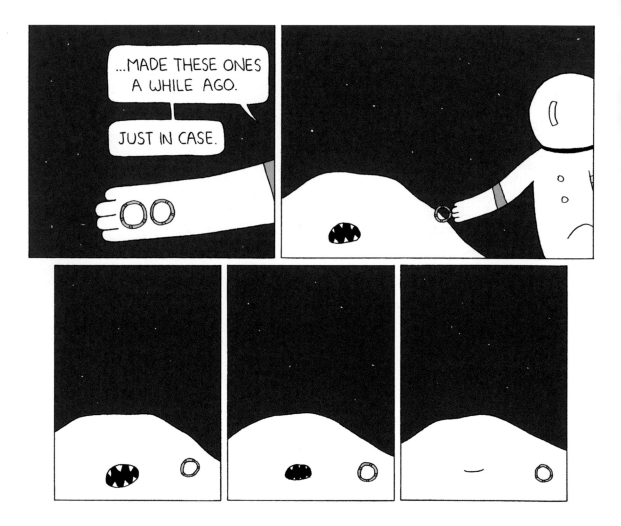

III

HEAVY STUFF

THE OPTIMIST AND THE REALIST

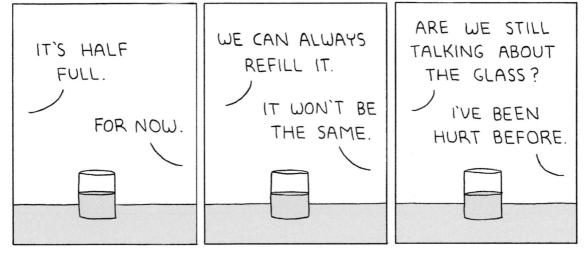

THE HISTORY OF MAN
WHAT THE HELL IS HAPPENING...
THE END

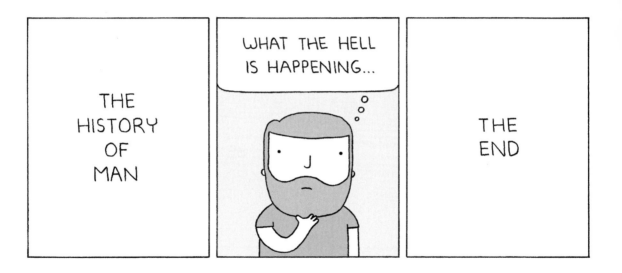

IN THE BEGINNING THERE WAS NOTHING
THEN HEAT
LIGHT
MATTER
A... SHOE
WHOSE FUCKING SHOE IS THAT?
SEAN, ARE YOU SERIOUS?
MY BAD.
YOU'RE RUINING EVERYTHING
JUST CHILL, DUDE.
I HAVE TO START OVER NOW
CAN YOU NOT BE A DICK ABOUT IT?

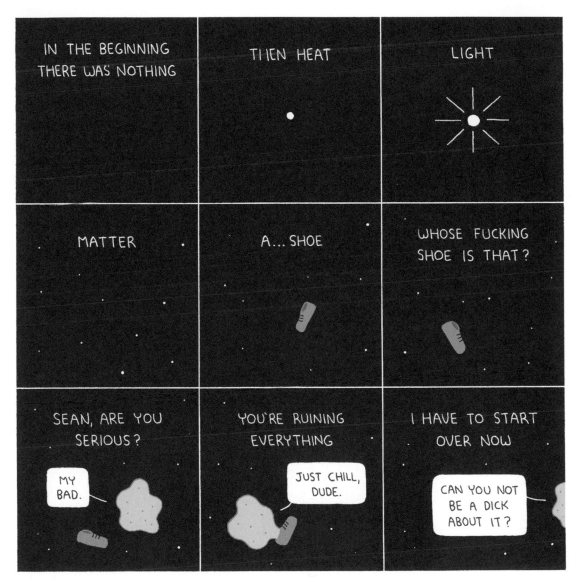

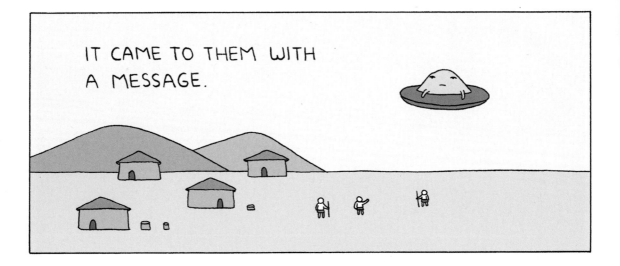

IT CAME TO THEM WITH
A MESSAGE.

BUT THEY COULD NOT
UNDERSTAND ITS ALIEN LANGUAGE

TRY TO WORK TOGETHER AND RESPECT EACH OTHER.
FUCKING WHAT?

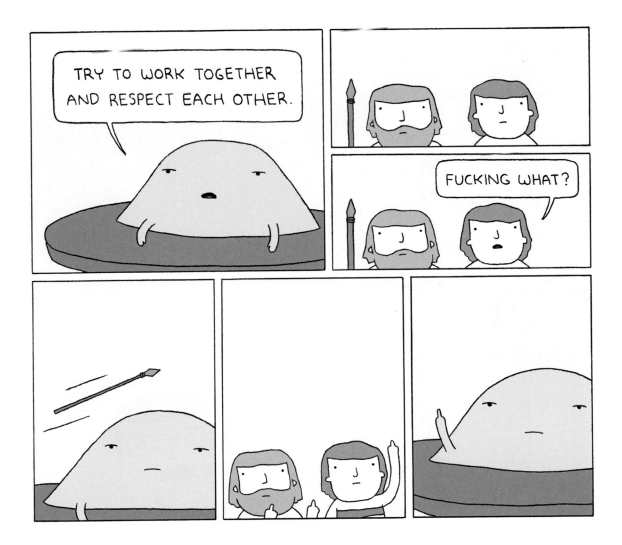

SON, ALWAYS HOPE FOR THE BEST AND PREPARE FOR THE WORST.
I GOT YOU THIS CONFETTI.
AND A GUN.
PARTY OR DIE, OKAY?
YES, PAPA.

BIRD on a
PLANE

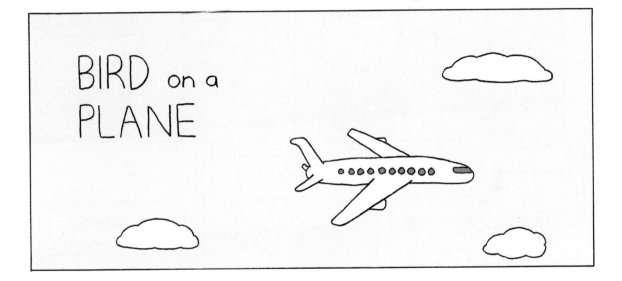

IT SEEMS KINDA WEIRD THAT YOU WOULD...
WHAT?
...USE A PLANE.
SIGH. I KNOW. IT'S JUST... I CAN'T BE AROUND OTHER BIRDS OUT THERE.
ARE YOU SHY?
NO.
I'M...
...AN ASSHOLE.
I'M AN ASSHOLE BIRD.

WHENEVER I'M AROUND OTHER BIRDS I JUST...
HELLO.

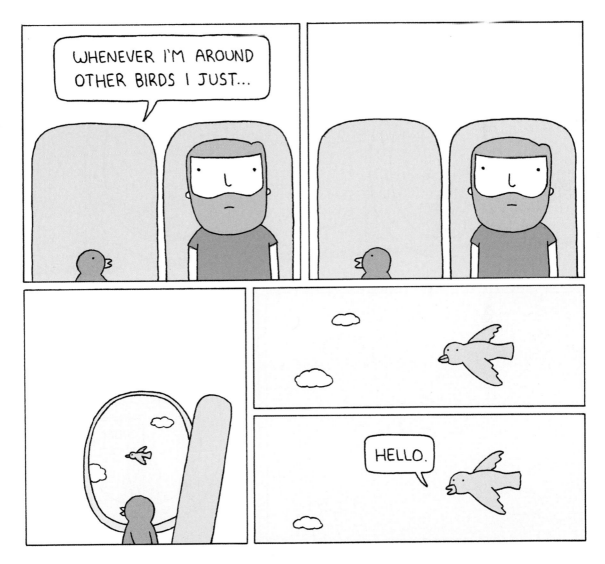

SIGH

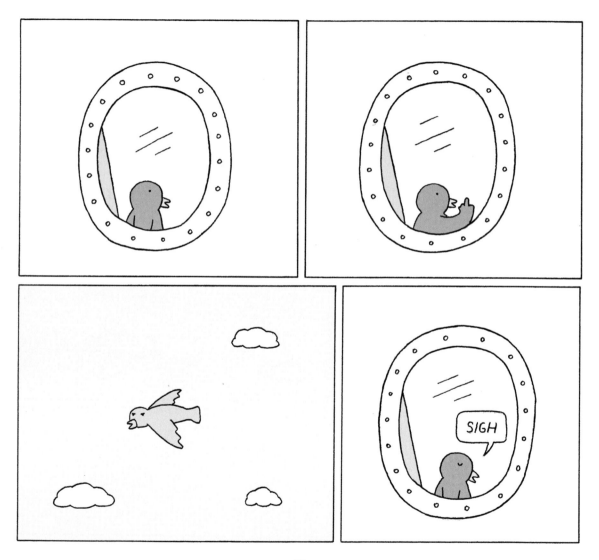

ASSHOLE BIRD
on a PLANE
SIGH

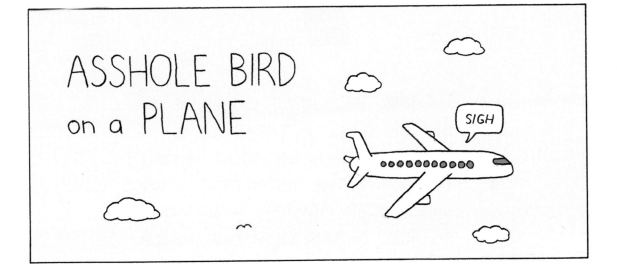

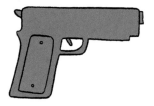

I THINK THE WORLD WOULD BE A
BETTER PLACE IF THERE WERE
NO GUNS. THEN WE COULD FINALLY
FOCUS ON THE IMPORTANT THINGS,
LIKE SWORD FIGHTING AND HOW
TO KILL A MAN WITH ONE PUNCH.

PEOPLE GET ANGRY AT THINGS THEY DON'T UNDERSTAND.
LIKE THIS WEIRDLY TALL FROG.
WHAT? HUH?!
HUUUUUUHH?!

SOMETHING POETIC ABOUT THE FUCKING RAIN

It's the first big rain in a long time. It smacks against the ground in alternating waves of torrential and slightly less torrential. It pings and pangs off of houses and lampposts, making a thousand different noises all at once, and I guess you could call it a "chorus of rain" or a "song of rain," but let's just call it fucking rain.

They were talking about this fucking rain for days.

"The rain is coming."

"It's going to rain."

"Did you hear?"

"About the rain?"

"Yeah, about the rain."

"Yeah, I heard. It's crazy."

And oh, is it crazy. People are crashing their cars like it's the cool thing to do, and the crashing gives way to the constant whine of emergency sirens. The sirens compete against the rain for loudest noise in the city, and the collective sounds come together to make a sort of "chorus of sounds."

I should also mention the wind, which is blowing with a tre-
mendous kind of windy arrogance. You should see what it's doing
to the trees, making them whip around and rock back and forth
with this unpredictable rhythm. It could be called something like
"a dance of trees" or "the graceful dance of the trees," but let's
just say these trees were shaking that shit like business was good.

So we've got all this stuff happening with the wind and the
rain and the noises that occur from them, and in the midst of it
all I find myself caught in this stupid mess of water and sound
halfway home from the supermarket. And though I'm soaked
completely, and though the supermarket didn't even have the
good kind of crunchy cinnamon cereal, I realize this is a time
to reflect on the beauty of stuff and the interconnectedness of
things. Like, this is it, you know? The rain and the noises working
in unison to communicate a perfect living energy, a reflection of
our very being—and then I slip on a coffee cup and submerge
most of my face in the gutter and the significance of the moment is quickly overcome by the taste of street water and what
is perhaps part of a Starbucks lid in my mouth.

OH NO
YOU DIED
AT LEAST I DON'T HAVE TO WORRY ABOUT BODY IMAGE ANYMORE.
OH HEY NEW GUY.

Everything is Fucked

IT'S TIME TO START THINKING ABOUT YOUR FUTURE
WHAT ARE YOUR GOALS?
HOW MANY OF THEM INVOLVE CHEESE?
Buy cheese
Eat cheese
Get a job
Be proactive
CAN YOU DO THE CHEESE ONES FIRST?
CAN YOU MAKE THE REST OF THEM INVOLVE CHEESE AS WELL?
Buy cheese
Eat cheese
Get ~~a job~~ CHEESE
Be ~~proactive~~ CHEESE

FUNNY BIRDIE

LIFE'S A BURDEN.
A BIRDEN.
HAHA

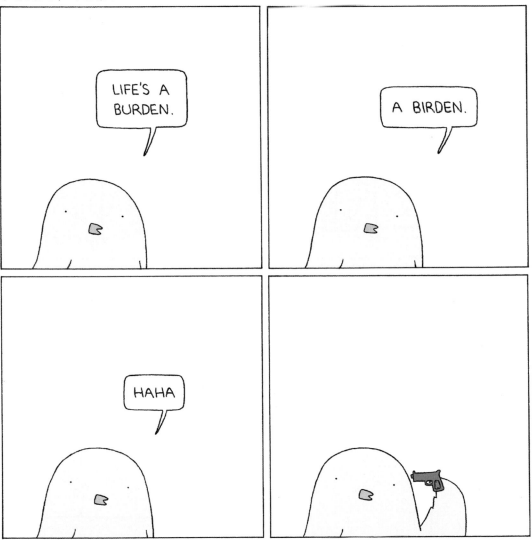

I HAVE ACHIEVED NOTHING IN LIFE.
BY ADMITTING THAT TO YOURSELF YOU HAVE ACHIEVED SOMETHING: SELF-AWARENESS.
I GUESS I AM PRETTY AWARE OF HOW USELESS I AM.
SEE?
YOU'RE RIGHT! I FEEL LIKE I CAN TAKE ON THE WORLD NOW!
BUT YOU WON'T.
DEFINITELY NOT.

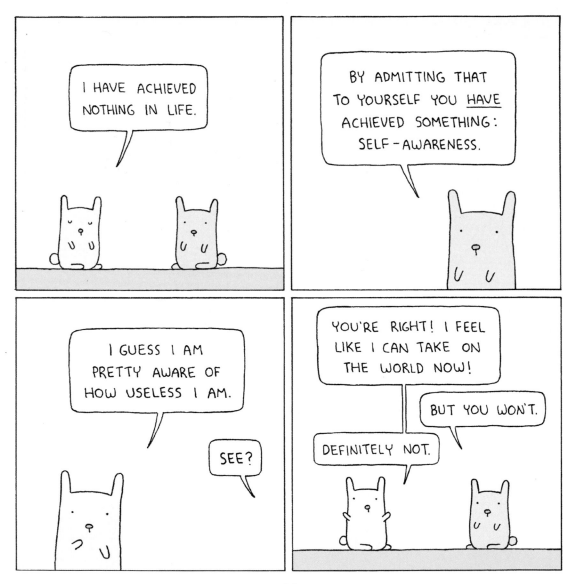

LISTEN TO YOUR ELDERS.
THEY OFFER KNOWLEDGE
AND WISDOM THAT ONLY
THE YEARS CAN BRING.

NOT PAUL, THOUGH.

PAUL IS A FUCKING LIAR.

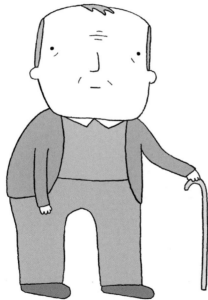

WILL WE FIND INTELLIGENT LIFE?
COULD IT BE RIGHT HERE ON EARTH?
COULD IT BE THIS MAN?
I'M NOT RACIST BUT I MEAN—
THE SEARCH CONTINUES

PAPA'S DEATHBED

"Amy, come here."

"What is it, Dad?"

"Your kid. The boy-child. What's his name?"

"Tommy."

"Tommy the Boy-Child."

"Just Tommy."

"Does he have a nickname?"

"We call him Buddy sometimes."

"Like he's your little friend."

"He's our little buddy, yeah."

"I want you to give him this. My father made it."

"This is a knife taped to a gun."

"My father was a poor craftsman."

"How did you get this into the hospital?"

"What have I told you, Amy?"

"Never ask about your weapons."

"That's right. Just give it to Buddy."

"Dad, he's five."

"Keep it for him until he's seven."

"Okay."

"I love you, Amy."

"I love you too, Dad."

"Oh actually wait— Give this one to your daughter."

"How many guns do you have here?"

"What did we just talk about?"

"I know, I know."

"Like twelve or thirty, though."

"Jesus, Dad."

"What have I taught you, Amy?"

"You never know when you're going to have to pistol-whip a male nurse."

"That's right."

"You've taught me so much, Dad. I'm going to miss you."

"What have I taught you, Amy?"

"Never miss a dying man or he'll haunt you and criticize your shoes."

"That's right."

"That one is weird, though."

"Yeah, my father taught me that one. He was a strange man."

"I can tell by the knife-gun."

"Ha ha. Family, right?"

Amy nodded. She looked down at the knife-gun in her lap and felt a lump in her throat. She fought back the tears and thought of Buddy, picturing the day she would give her son the heirloom.

"Family," she said, smiling as she watched her father glare suspiciously at a male nurse in the hallway.

WHEN YOU'RE YOUNG YOU THINK YOU'LL LIVE FOREVER.
UNLESS YOU'RE THIS BABY.
WHO IS ACUTELY AWARE OF HIS OWN MORTALITY.
A-"CUTE"-LY, RIGHT? HAHA.

YOU TOO SHALL BE FOOD FOR THE WORMS.
SHIT, BABY.

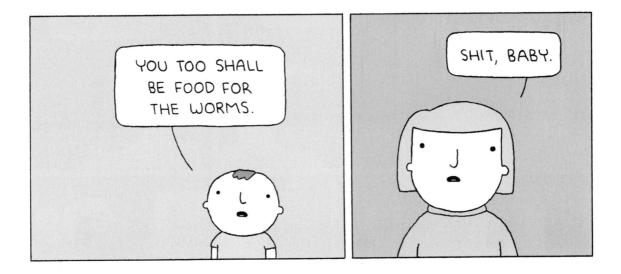

SO-DEEP SPACE

DO YOU THINK WE'LL FIND LIFE OUT HERE?
EVERYTHING IS LIFE, MAN.
OH MY GOD. YOU'RE RIGHT, JIM.
NASA, JIM DID IT. WE'RE COMING HOME.
ARE YOU BEING SARCASTIC?
WHY DO YOU THINK THAT?

DAD, HOW DO I GROW A BEARD LIKE YOU?
YOU JUST HAVE TO BELIEVE, SON.

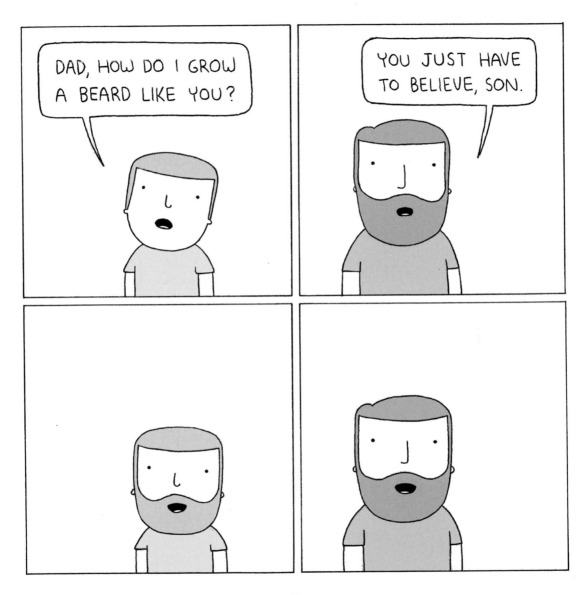

ERNESTO, HOW DO I GET YOUR HAMSTER TO LIKE ME?
HE HAS TO TRUST YOU. TELL HIM A SECRET.
I'M AFRAID NO ONE WILL REMEMBER ME WHEN I'M GONE.
MAN, THAT WAS WAY TOO REAL. YOU'RE GONNA FREAK HIM OUT.
SHOOT, SORRY.

HE'S THINKING ABOUT LIFE NOW, GREAT JOB.
SORRY, DUDE.
HE'S NOT SURE ABOUT THINGS ANYMORE.
MY BAD.

FLOWER, HOW DOES IT FEEL TO BE A SYMBOL OF LOVE?
LOVE? HA!
LOOK AT ME. WITHERING AWAY HERE.
MY LIFE IS A GLIMPSE AT THE UNRELENTING MARCH OF TIME, FOOL.
MY PRESENCE IS A CONSTANT REMINDER OF YOUR OWN MORTALITY.
I'M A SYMBOL OF DEATH.
I'M THE ULTIMATE BADASS.
OOH, PRETTY PETALS.
DAMN YOU! FEAR MY SYMBOLISM!

FLUFFY MADE HIS
OWN LUCK.

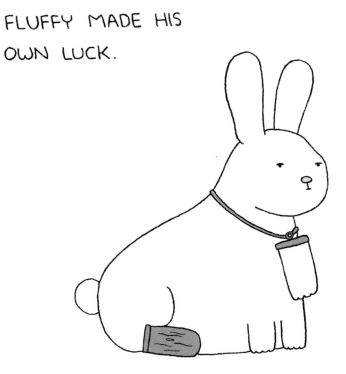

WE SHOULDN'T FORGET WHERE WE COME FROM. WE WERE TREES ONCE.
DON'T CLING TO THE PAST, JOHN. YOU'LL END UP LIKE ARTHUR.
DAMN.
WONDERFUL DAY IN THE FOREST, EH, BOYS?
YES, WONDERFUL, ARTHUR.

DAD, CAN I GO PLAY?
NOT UNTIL YOU DISCERN THE MEANING OF YOUR EXISTENCE.
IT'S... UH...

MAYBE THERE'S MORE TO LIFE THAN STANDING BEHIND BABIES AT IKEA

I'm not complaining. God knows the world isn't perfect and it's not like I'm being marched to my death in a desert somewhere. But right now there are seven babies taking up this entire aisle at IKEA and I'm beginning to feel like there has to be more to it all than this.

Again, not complaining. I'm in a clean, well-lit space. I'm warm. I'm not hungry or tired and I've lived well for a long time. But each of these babies has its own stroller, and this aisle is only a few feet wide, and I can't help but think there's a big part of life that I'm missing out on.

I should try to be grateful, I know. Appreciate what I have. Wise men teach us to live in the present, and my present is colored in neutral shades of beige and gray—tastefully Swedish and totally unobjectionable. But there are nine babies now and I doubt that they planned to come here together. I doubt that they could organize something like that, so I know somewhere nearby there are nine young couples talking about the benefits of lamps, totally unaware of what they've created here and that a stroller is essentially a car for babies, and that nine stopped cars is essentially a traffic jam in fucking basically every road-faring culture.

But really, I know I should focus on the positives. The air is cool and it smells like new furniture. I can look at the living room displays and pretend that I live in one. I can pretend I have kids of my own and they sit at their little display computers and they say, "Why don't we have real computers, Daddy?" and I tell them not to ask about such things. I know some people don't even have fake living rooms and imaginary families, and I know I should be grateful, but one of these babies just looked at me from his stroller, and I swear to god mouthed "fuck you" and I just feel like there has to be a bigger world out there somewhere.

ARE YOU SURE YOU SHOULD EAT THAT?
IS ANYONE REALLY SURE OF ANYTHING?
I GUESS NOT.
ARE YOU SURE ABOUT THAT?
I... DAMN, SHIT IS COMPLICATED.

YOU'RE A SMART GUY, ALLEN.
ALLEN?

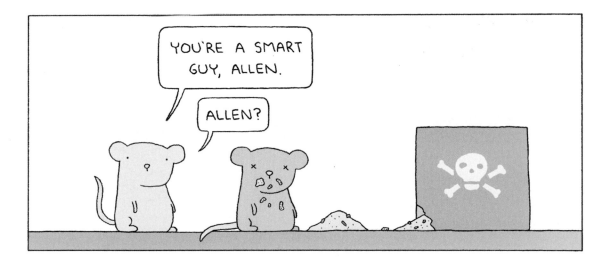

I NEED TO BE MORE CONFIDENT.
YOU JUST HAVE TO NOT CARE, YOU KNOW? JUST BE COOL.
LIKE, LOOK AT TOMÁS.
GOD, HE'S COOL.
HE IS DISGUSTINGLY COOL.

TOMÁS, YOU DISGUST ME.
I HATE YOU, TOMÁS.
LET'S HANG OUT.
YOU ASSHOLE.
DOES TOMORROW WORK?
I'M GOING TO THROW UP ON YOU.

CHOOSE YOUR WEAPON!

MY MIND.
MY SWORDS.
AAAHHHH!
HAVE I MADE A POOR DECISION?

15TH CENTURY DAD

KIDS, I'M GOING TO DISCOVER AMERICA.

DAD, THEY ALREADY DISCOVERED AMERICA.

THEN I'M GOING TO DISCOVER MYSELF.

HAHA, THE BUNNY FOUND A BOOK.
IT'S LIKE HE'S EDUCATING HIMSELF.
WHAT IF HE WANTS CIVIL RIGHTS NOW?
THOSE ARE DANGEROUS THOUGHTS, BUNNY.

SOAP

When I lived in the city I went to a Laundromat called Lavanderia, which is Spanish for "Laundromat." I liked that they were straightforward about the name. There was another Laundromat across the street called Sparkle Time. It was a stupid place.

Lavanderia wasn't trying to impress anyone. It contained two rows of washing machines, two rows of dryers, a television, and a small woman named Pilar. Pilar was the manager, and she had earned a reputation on the block for being a hard-ass. A teenager once snuck into the Laundromat and stole Pilar's Cheetos, and she said she would kill him with his skateboard. My neighbor Tanya told me Pilar was a "bad bitch." A lot of songs say this is essentially the best type of bitch.

For a petite lady who favored high-waisted jeans, Pilar was an imposing figure. She stood straight and smiled sparingly. When she walked she kept one hand on her hip and the other poised to jab an accusatory finger at anyone caught abusing the facilities. There was something in the way her neck moved that suggested a bird of prey. I don't know the context, but I once saw her stare down a stray dog in the parking lot.

When Pilar wasn't in action she leaned against the wall and

watched Spanish soap operas on the television. The shows seemed to calm her, and during these times she appeared noticeably less angry. I asked her once if she liked soap operas because she worked around soap so much, and she told me I was an *idiota*, which is Spanish for "very funny person."

Even though she loved my jokes, I knew Pilar wasn't there to make friends. Like the troubled protagonists of her telenovelas, she seemed to relish confrontation. I started to wonder if this wasn't just an act she put on to get through the day. I wondered if she was a sweet and quiet woman under her brash exterior and if she saved the best parts of herself for the people she actually cared about. I wondered these things until one morning, a week before I left the city, when I saw Pilar throw a boy's skateboard into the street while yelling at him in Spanish. The only word I recognized was "Cheetos," but it was clear that Pilar did not fuck around, and that some people are just born to be bad bitches.

YOU MIGHT FEEL SAD SOMETIMES.
BUT JUST REMEMBER...
NOTHING IS PERMANENT.

ALL THAT EXISTS WILL
FADE TO DUST.

AND SEEP INTO
THE ANONYMOUS
VOID OF ETERNITY.

DO YOU FEEL BETTER?

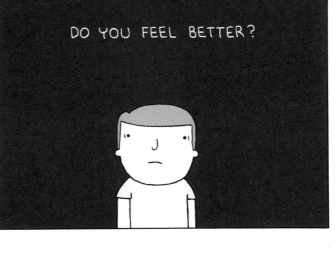

DINOSAURS WERE JUST LIKE US

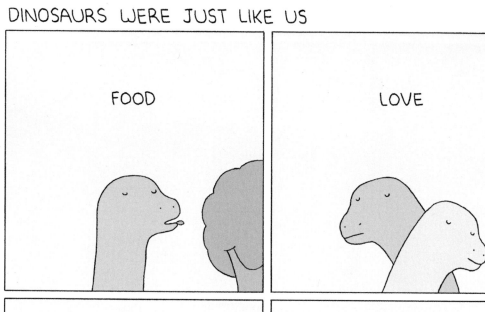

FOOD

LOVE

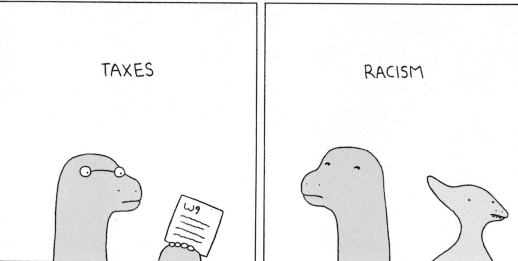

TAXES

RACISM

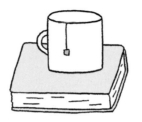

WHEN IT'S COLD OUTSIDE I LIKE TO
CURL UP WITH A THICK BOOK AND
A HOT CUP OF TEA. THEN I LIKE TO
USE THE BOOK AS A COASTER FOR
THE TEA AND BROWSE THE INTERNET
ON MY LAPTOP WHILE SIMULTANEOUSLY
TEXTING MY FRIENDS AND FLIPPING
BETWEEN CHANNELS ON TELEVISION.

WHAT WERE WE TALKING ABOUT AGAIN?

MY BLT!
IT'S OKAY, DUDE. EVERYTHING HAPPENS FOR A REASON.
OH REALLY, KEVIN? DO INNOCENT PEOPLE DIE IN WAR FOR A REASON?
UH...
DID GENERAL MILLS CHANGE THE COOKIE CRISP RECIPE AND MAKE IT COMPLETELY SHITTY FOR A REASON?

WELL...
NO! THERE ARE NO REASONS. THE UNIVERSE IS COLD AND UNCARING AND EVERYONE WILL DIE AND NO ONE WILL HAVE COOKIE CEREAL AND THERE'S NOTHING WE CAN DO ABOUT IT.
PECK PECK

IV

UNEXPLAINED EVENTS

I GUESS I'M A DOG PERSON.
GUESS AGAIN.
YOU PIECE OF SHIT...

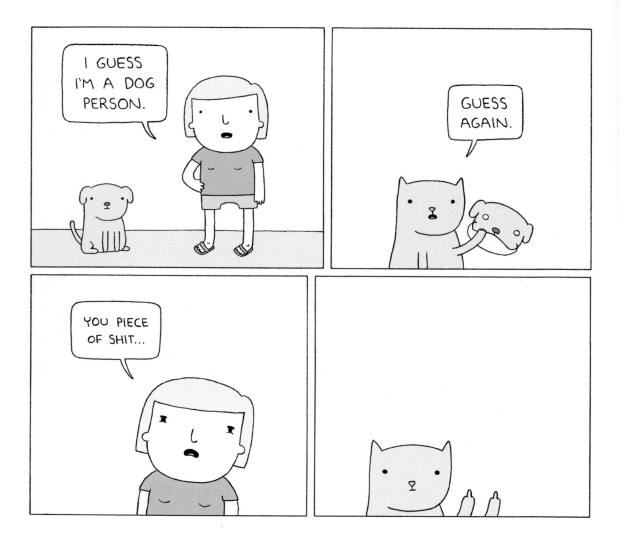

VARIOUS HAUNTED/OBSOLETE MEDIA

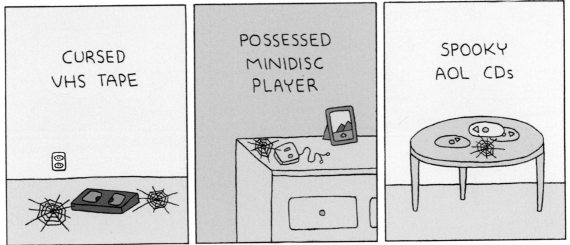

CURSED
VHS TAPE

POSSESSED
MINIDISC
PLAYER

SPOOKY
AOL CDs

DON'T FEED THE MONSTER

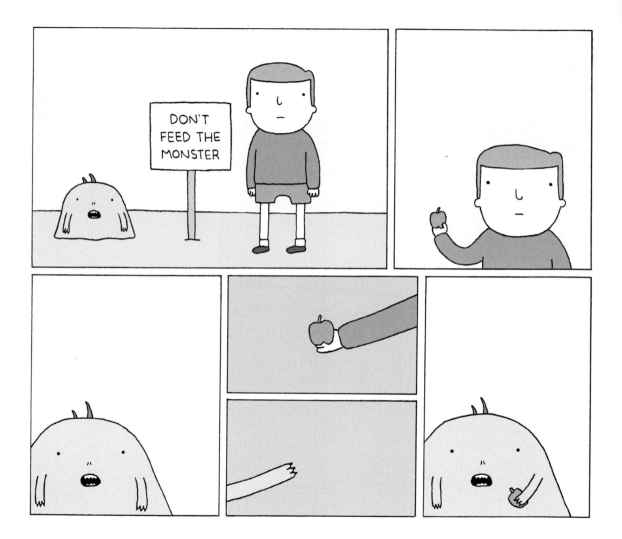

ASSHOLE.

DON'T FEED THE MONSTER
HE IS UNGRATEFUL

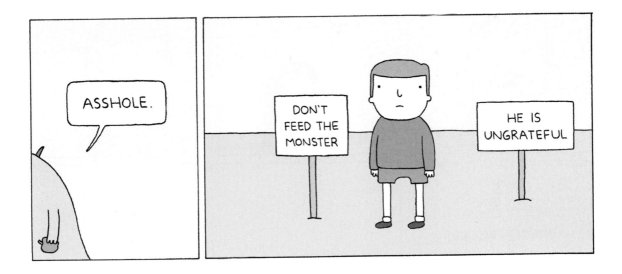

NO RESPECT FOR DEATH-GOOSE

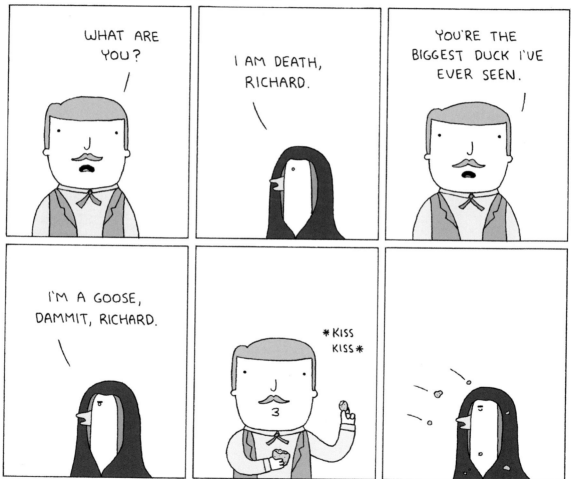

HOW OLD IS YOUR BABY?
37

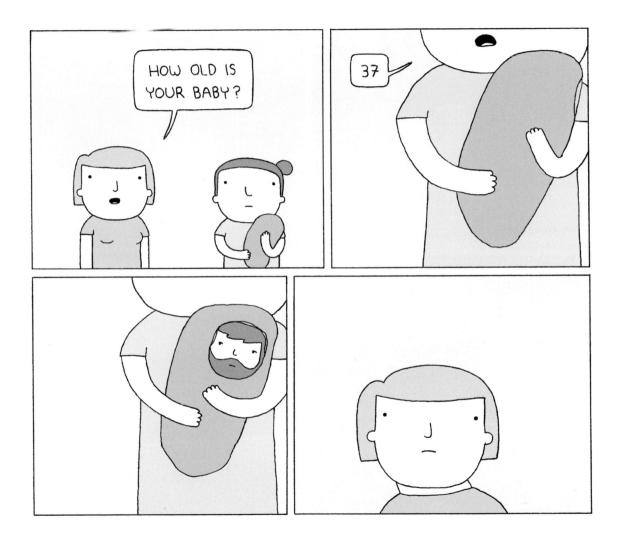

THE CITY COMES ALIVE AT NIGHT
AND DANCES BENEATH THE DARKENED SKY WITH A WILD AND PULSATING ENERGY
FEW SURVIVE
IT IS AN UNDESIRABLE LOCATION

THE DOG IS DIGGING HOLES ALL OVER THE YARD.
DON'T BE SO QUICK TO JUDGE.
OH, HE'S ACTUALLY TRAPPING SMALLER ANIMALS.
AND INTRODUCING THEM TO DRUGS.
THIS IS NOT BETTER.

GHOST FRIEND

ARE YOU HAUNTING ME?
I THOUGHT WE COULD JUST HANG OUT.
CAN YOU NOT DO THAT THING WITH THE CAT THEN?
SORRY.

AND THE WALLS.
YOU DIE
SORRY SORRY
AND THE CAT AGAIN.
MY BAD.

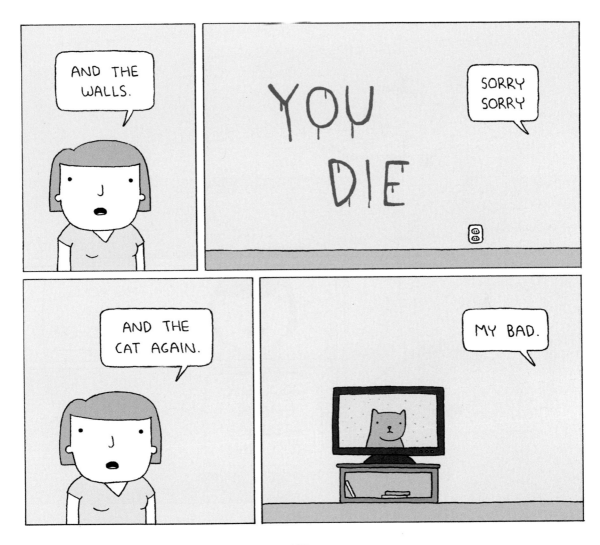

UURRR
THE FOUL BEAST APPROACHES!
WOW, OKAY. I HAVE. FEELINGS TOO, MAN.

OH, I...
I DON'T NEED YOUR JUDGMENT, YOU KNOW?
HATER.

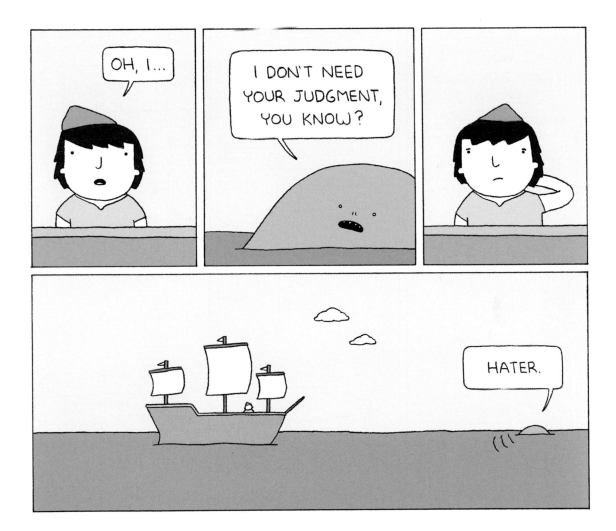

THE HOLES IN THAT BOX LOOK LIKE A SUSPICIOUS FACE.
TOO SUSPICIOUS...

EARNEST EARLY HAD VERY BIG EARS.
THEY SAID HE COULD HEAR A MOUSE SNEAKING UP FROM A HUNDRED YARDS AWAY.
HE COULD NOT.

NEW MATTRESS

"Hi. Can I help you?"

"Yeah, I saw in an ad that this mattress will give me the sleep of a thousand angels?"

"Yes, that's right."

"What does that mean, exactly?"

"You'll be imbued with the memories of a thousand immortal souls, your mind flowing freely between this plane and the next as you experience an infinite cycle of birth and rebirth across the seas of ascension and into the undying consciousness."

"And that comes with a memory foam topper?"

"The topper is extra."

"Oh that's extra?"

"It's fifty dollars extra."

"Do you have any that come with the topper included?"

"The SleepRest 400 comes with a topper."

"And does it do the undying consciousness thing?"

"No, but it contours to fit your sleeping position. It's very nice."

"That sounds nice."

"Should I ring you up, then?"

"Yes, thanks."

OH GOD, I'VE BECOME MY MOTHER.
SHE WAS ALWAYS TRANSFORMING INTO A BIRD.
KAREN
MOM?
YOU DISAPPOINT ME.
OH GOD

WHO IS THIS BABY?
BABY, WHO ARE YOU?
MYSTERIOUS

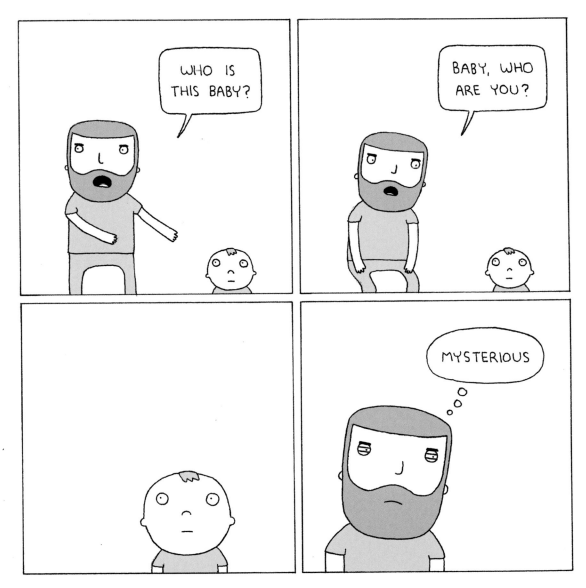

I AIN'T DEAD YET
YOU BEEN DEAD, LIKE, 3,000 YEARS.
SHIT MAN WHAT

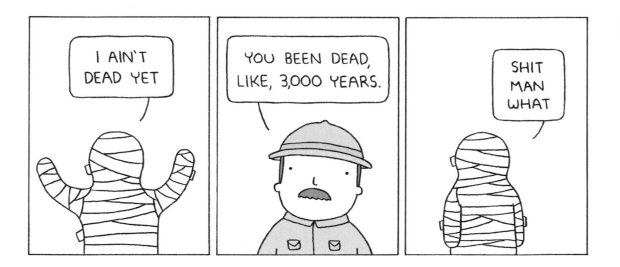

BREAKFAST IN BED

"Who wants breakfast in bed?" Chloe asks as she enters the room carrying a tray.

"I do!" Russell replies, sitting up in bed.

Chloe trips. The tray falls from her hands. It hits the floor and the breakfast spills across the carpet. The breakfast is everywhere.

"Well, at least you still got breakfast in bed," Chloe says as she points to a spot of breakfast on the duvet.

"Chloe, this is foolish," Russell says. "This is not the type of breakfast in bed that you initially referred to."

"I know, but—"

"Why would you change the definition of the breakfast like that?"

"I just—"

"I can't do this anymore."

Russell stands up. He wipes breakfast from his arm and gathers his things. He leaves. Chloe cries as she stares at the breakfast and wonders where it all went wrong.

—

"Who wants breakfast in bed?" Chloe asks as she enters the room carrying a tray.

"I do!" Russell replies, sitting up in bed.

Chloe trips. The tray falls from her hands. The breakfast leaps into the air and spins acrobatically, rearranging itself in midflight. The tray clatters to the floor and the breakfast lands perfectly on its plate, as if nothing has happened at all. Russell stares wide-eyed.

"Chloe, how did . . . What the . . ."

"I don't know," Chloe says. "I just . . ."

Russell begins to shake.

"How the fuck how the fuck," he repeats over and over again.

"Oh my god."

"Did you see it spin acrobatically?"

"Oh my god oh my god."

Chloe runs from the room screaming. Russell slowly begins to shit himself as the breakfast stares menacingly from the floor.

—

"Who wants breakfast in bed?" Chloe asks as she enters the room carrying a tray.

"I do!" Russell replies, sitting up in bed.

Chloe trips. The tray falls from her hands. Elsewhere a child laughs for the first time. A bat soars through a jungle in Peru. The Earth turns and a star in a distant galaxy burns brightly against the emptiness of space before it is obscured by an indiscernible black mass that drifts silently through the cosmos. Millions of worlds dissolve in its path. Countless lives blink out in an instant.

"I'll go make some more," Chloe says.

"Thanks. I'll clean this up," Russell replies.

"Thanks, babe."

I'M NOT THAT GOOD WITH PEOPLE.
PRACTICE ON ME. HOW WOULD YOU INTRODUCE YOURSELF?
YOU'VE OFFERED ME A CHAIR. THAT'S A GOOD START.
LET'S BACK UP A COUPLE STEPS.

EXCUSE ME, MISS?
DO YOU NEED A BABY?
I FOUND THIS ONE.
WHAT SORT OF FEATURES DOES IT HAVE?
ARMS. LEGS. SOME HAIR.

GPS?
THAT'S NOT REALLY A TYPICAL THING BABIES HAVE.
NEVER MIND.

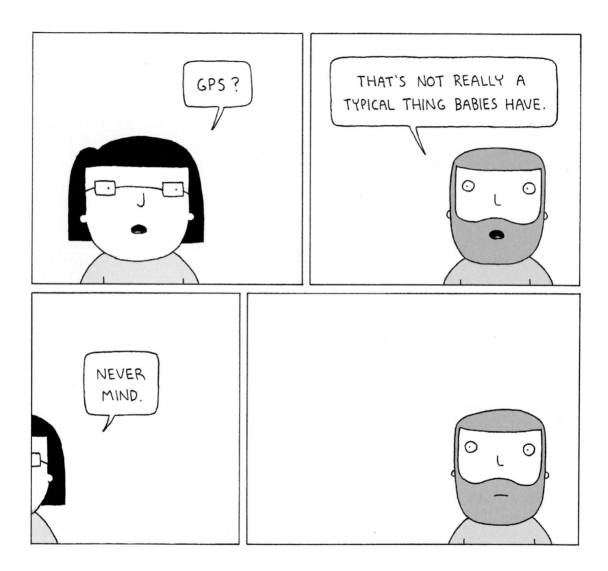

Free baby
Good condition
Now with
GPS
+
iTunes

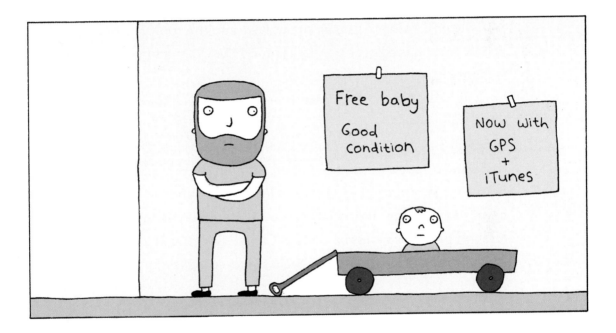

THE WORST THING

"Oh my god," Cheryl said as she walked into the room. "Justin spilled soda in the kitchen and it's literally the worst thing ever."

Tom looked up from his phone.

"Oh really, Cheryl?" he asked sarcastically. "Is it literally the worst thing ever?"

He stood and walked into the kitchen. It was on fire. The soda had gained sentience and was strangling Justin with telekinetic powers. A swarm of bees encircled Tom and he choked as they flew down his throat and stung at his eyes. He struggled to scream through the smoke and the bees as Cheryl sat in the living room and texted Sarah, who literally could not even believe how cray this shit was.

AT THE MUSEUM...

WHAT ARE YOU DOING, DUDE?
I'M REGARDING THIS ART PIECE WITH SUSPICION.
I REGARD ANYTHING I DON'T UNDERSTAND WITH SUSPICION, JUST IN CASE.
I GUESS THAT DOESN'T SOUND COMPLETELY CRAZY.
HEY, WHAT ARE YOU GUYS DO—
WHOA, WHAT THE HELL IS THAT?

V

FRIENDS, FEELINGS, LOVERS, AND PEOPLE

SOME PEOPLE SEEM TO HAVE IT ALL. BUT LOOK CLOSER...
FULL OF PAST-DUE BILLS
LEASED ON CREDIT
NOT A REAL DOG

DO YOU LIKE PIZZA?
DOES A BEAR LIKE TO DO ITS BUSINESS IN THE WOODS?
I LIKE PIZZA
THIS IS NICE.

COMPUTER, PLAY A SONG.
BEEP BOOP BEEP
THAT'S NOT VERY GOOD, COMPUTER.
I KNOW, I WAS KIDDING. HAHA.
HAHA.

LATER...

YOU THINK YOU'RE A MUSICIAN?
CRASH!

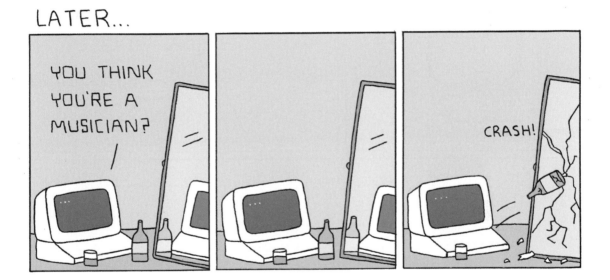

YOU'RE BEAUTIFUL, CHEESEBURGER.
NAH GIRL, YOU'RE BEAUTIFUL.
TEE HEE
TAKE YOUR SHIRT OFF.
WHAT

"WHAT'S WRONG, MOON?" ASKED THE EARTH.
"I AM LONELY," SAID THE MOON.
"WE'LL TAKE CARE OF THAT," SAID THE EARTH.
"OH SHIT," SAID THE HORSE.

ERNESTO, YOU GOT A FRIEND REQUEST.
A WHAT?
IT'S A REQUEST FOR FRIENDSHIP.
FROM...

ANTHONY.
ANTHONY WALRUS
CONFIRM?
YES
NO
HE'D LIKE SOME OF YOUR FRIENDSHIP.
HOW MUCH FRIENDSHIP DO I HAVE TO GIVE HIM?
NOT A LOT. BARELY ANY AT ALL, ACTUALLY.
HE MIGHT TRY TO GIVE YOU SOME OF HIS FRIENDSHIP, THOUGH.

OH GOD. THAT JUST... SOUNDS LIKE A LOT TO DEAL WITH.
I KNOW, I KNOW.
WHY DOES THIS HAVE TO HAPPEN TO ME?
YOU COULD JUST IGNORE IT.
YES, YES! IGNORE IT.
IGNORING IT.

ELSEWHERE...

ERNESTO
REQUEST PENDING
THERE'S STILL A CHANCE...

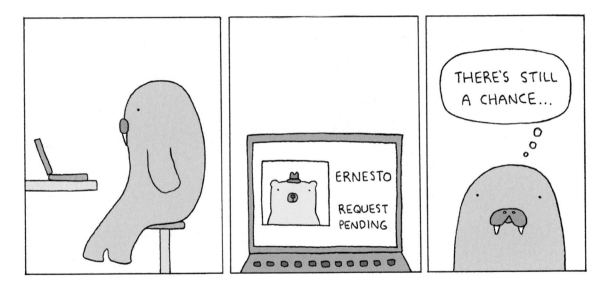

INTERNET DATE

Erica87
hey

BDan2
hi ☺

Erica87
your profile says you're into model boats

BDan2
?

Erica87
model boats and cocaine

BDan2
"models, boats, and cocaine"

Erica 87
oh

BDan2
yeah

Erica87
nm

LOVE-DUCK, THE PROTECTOR

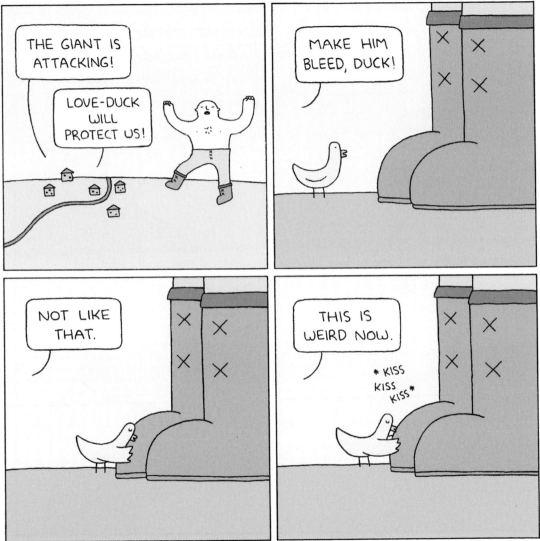

STEREOTYPE

CAN I SEE SOME MAGIC?
WHAT, BECAUSE I'M A WIZARD I KNOW MAGIC?
Racist

USE YOUR HANDS IN CONVERSATION TO HELP PROJECT CONFIDENCE.
HELLO, JONATHAN.
SLAP
SLAP
SLAP
SLAP
SLAP

NOTHING IS BAD IN FRIENDSHIP TOWN
THE TREES ARE KIND
THE SQUIRRELS ARE KIND
THE CLOUDS ARE KIND

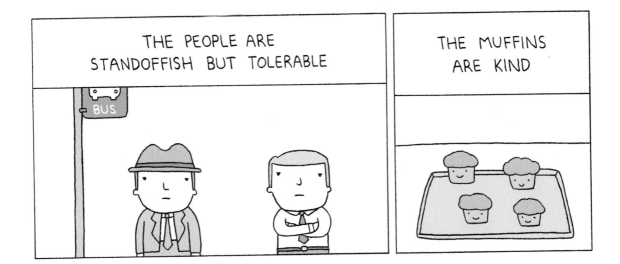

THE PEOPLE ARE
STANDOFFISH BUT TOLERABLE

BUS

THE MUFFINS
ARE KIND

CHECKOUT

Hello, supermarket employee whose checkout line I've chosen today. I'd just like to run through a few things with you before we get started.

1. I've brought my own bag, which I will place on the checkout counter and stare at for a few moments while I decide whether I should attempt to bag my own groceries.
2. I will decide that bagging my own groceries is the proper thing to do in this situation, as you will be occupied with scanning the remainder of my items, and I will think that I am being helpful.
3. I will ruin everything. I will put the eggs at the bottom of the bag and drop several loose onions on top of them, followed by a loaf of bread and a rotisserie chicken, which I will tip sideways in the bag so the juices run down on top of the eggs and the onions.

4. You will throw a number of sidelong glances in my direction as I follow the chicken with a tube of toothpaste, a roll of aluminum foil, and a half-gallon of milk.

5. The chicken juices will begin to seep through the bag.

6. I will turn to swipe my credit card, giving you enough time to take everything out of the bag and rearrange it while I furrow my brow and concentrate very hard on signing my name. I will make it the best signature I have ever done. I will see the chicken juice from the corner of my eye and I will double down on my name-signing efforts.

7. I will finally look up and jokingly compare the bagging pro-cess to the video game *Tetris*. You will smile a very small amount and I will be disappointed in myself.

8. You will hand me my receipt. Our transaction will end. The smell of chicken will be apparent.

HEY DUDE, WHAT DO YOU THINK OF THESE SHORTS?
THEY'RE REALLY HIGH UP.
YEAH, THAT'S THE STYLE.
YOU LOOK LIKE A GERMAN CHILD WEARING THE TRADITIONAL COSTUME OF HIS PEOPLE.

THAT'S...
REALLY SPECIFIC.
LIKE A TRADITIONAL
GERMAN CHILD.
ALL RIGHT MAN,
WHATEVER.
LATER...
DID HE
LIKE THEM?
NOT NOW, HANS.

HOW WILL YOU EXPRESS YOURSELF?
WITH HATS
THROUGH DANCE
MY 'STACHE
MY ART
HIS ART

THESE PANTS
NO PANTS
RAP
ROCK
ROCKS
ATTENTION-GRABBING SOCKS

MR. TURTLE, THAT'S DANGEROUS.
YOU GOTTA LEARN TO HANDLE A PIECE.
POW
POW
POW POW POW POW

POW
POW
POW
POW
POW
POW

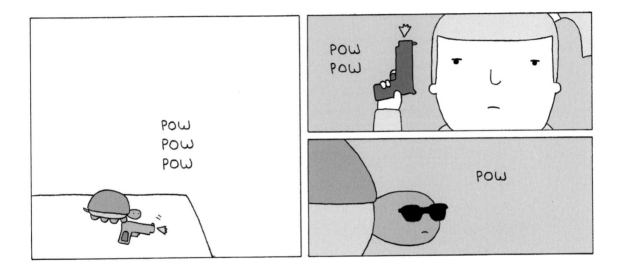

LET'S NOT JUMP TO CONCLUSIONS ABOUT THE GUY WITH THE SWORD

So yeah, this guy just walked into the coffee shop with a sword and I get how that probably seems weird. He's not wearing a shirt and he has a tattoo of a gun on his face, so obviously the whole thing is sort of different from the usual Starbucks vibe. But everyone just needs to chill, all right? I know a couple of you live in the suburbs and aren't used to a dynamic culture, but this is the city and we do things a little differently here.

Anyway, I'm glad we could meet to talk strategy. Heather's been working on our new mobile campaign and— All right, Heather, I see you looking at the guy with the sword again. Are you that sheltered? Yes, thank you for pointing out that he has a second, larger tattoo, which is, in fact, a scar where he apparently scrawled the word "blood" across his chest with a knife. A lot of cultures encourage body modification, and basically everyone in the office has ink, okay? It's the city, Heather.

And Thomas, stop muttering fearfully about his eyes. Some people naturally have a detached, glazed-over look that suggests a lingering break from reality. Great observation, detective. You too, Heather, highlighting for us once again that the guy has drawn his sword and is crouching in attack position while repeatedly shouting, "Ninja revolution!" You should compare notes with Thomas, who is now running for the exit with the rest of these tourists like he's never even been in a city before.

IT'S SAD HOW THE PHRASE "THANKS A LOT" HAS BECOME SO ASSOCIATED WITH SARCASM.
OOH BAGELS. THANKS A LOT, TED.
FUCK YOU TOO, SUSAN.

WISH YOU WERE TALLER?

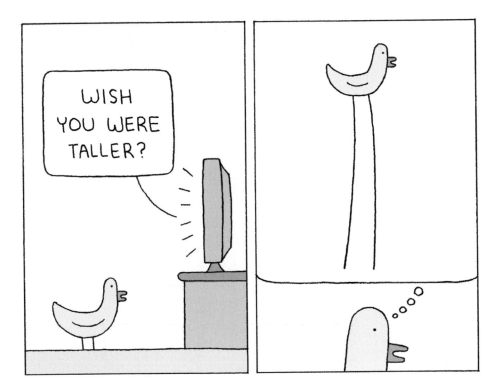

YOU NEED SOMETHING TO DEFINE YOUR STYLE.
HOW ABOUT I'M ALWAYS EATING A QUESADILLA?
BUT JUST REALLY CASUAL ABOUT IT, YOU KNOW?
YEAH, THAT'S GOOD.

LOOKING GOOD
WITH THAT
QUESADILLA

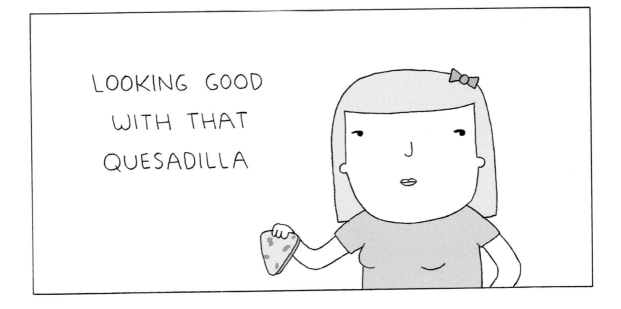

DON'T LOOK AT ME WHILE I FINISH THIS CANTALOUPE

I know you see me, Ryan. I know you're sitting there across from me, pretending to speak with Sarah about your new phone, but I see that little glance and I know you're watching me reach for the cantaloupe again.

Seven. I've had seven pieces of cantaloupe, Ryan. Look at the chewed-out rinds glazing over in a haphazard stack on my paper plate. Count them. Count them and judge me as you look toward the cantaloupe bowl and then down at your napkin, which you're using as a plate because you've had only two slices and because your game is fucking weak, Ryan.

I watched you too, you know. Saw you nibbling half-assedly on those thin slices, your tiny mouth like that of a feeble old rabbit. I'm a wolf, Ryan. I'm the wolf of the cantaloupe and I will eat it all and feel nothing of this shame you try to project at me because the wolf knows only the will to survive and to eat the cantaloupe.

Look at the bowl now, Ryan. Look with your watery rabbit eyes. We're down to the last slice.

What was that? Did you just move your arm? Are you going

for it? Let me take a moment to tell you this is a very poor idea. Did I mention I'm a wolf? And like a wolf I move with stunning speed, my claws extending toward the bowl and around the cantaloupe and back to my mouth in a single fluid motion. And then my teeth are sinking deep into the orange flesh and the juice is running freely from my gaping maw as you look on through the pain of your inevitable defeat with that sad rabbit face.

Look away, Ryan. You don't deserve to watch.

I'M SCARED OF HEIGHTS.
I'VE NEVER TOLD ANYONE THAT.
IT'S GOOD TO BE OPEN WITH PEOPLE.
I EAT MY NEPHEW'S BABY FOOD SOMETIMES, AND MY SISTER'S ALL "WHERE IS IT?" AND I'M LIKE, "I DON'T KNOW, BE A BETTER MOTHER."

DO YOU WANT A CROISSANT?
A WHAT?
YOU DON'T KNOW WHAT A CROISSANT IS?
IT'S A SORT OF ITALIAN VILLAGE.
I'M NOT OFFERING YOU AN ITALIAN VILLAGE.

ALLRIGHT, JUST GIVE IT TO ME.
THIS IS BREAD.
IT'S LIKE CULTURAL BREAD.
I FEEL SMART WHEN I EAT IT.
PECK PECK
YEAH, THAT'S THE POINT.

WHATUP, INTERNET.
#crusont

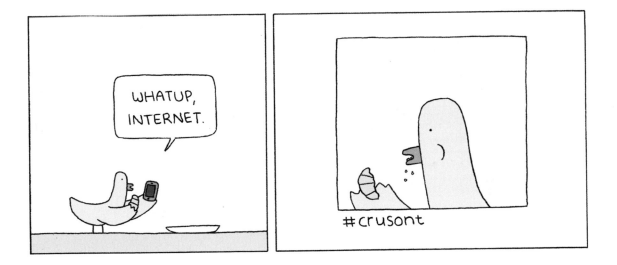

DINNER

Alexander stumbled into the dining room and grabbed the table to steady himself. Two vodkas, half a beer, and an empty stomach had rendered him quite wobbly, and his inebriated state was more than obvious to the others in the room.

"You're drunk, Alexander," his wife, Julia, said from her seat at the table.

"No, *you're* drunk," Alexander retorted.

It was true that Julia was also drunk. Her workload at the office had steadily increased over the past month, and her evening wine intake had risen along with it. She stood up swiftly and began to protest, but instead released a mighty belch, blushed, and sat back down.

"Mother, you're drunk," her daughter, Beth-Margaret, said.

"*You're* drunk, Beth-Margaret," Julia answered.

It was true that Beth-Margaret was also drunk. She and her best friend, Suzanne, had attended the high school basketball game earlier that evening, bringing with them a plastic water bottle filled with gin that they had taken from Suzanne's mother's liquor cabinet. It had been a thrilling act of rebellion.

"You're drunk, Beth-Margaret," Beth-Margaret's younger brother, Robbie, quipped from his seat beside her.

"*You're* drunk, Robbie," Beth-Margaret hiccupped.

It was true that Robbie was also drunk. He had just turned six, and the pressures of first grade were beginning to wear on him. His age showed in his furrowed brow and his rumpled Star Wars pajamas.

"Bark, bark," Cha-Cha the family dog barked from beneath the table.

"No, *you're* drunk, Cha-Cha!" Robbie shouted.

It was true that Cha-Cha was also drunk. Cha-Cha was an alcoholic.

"We're worried about you, Cha-Cha," Alexander said.

"Shit, man," Cha-Cha barked.

"We love you and want to help you," Julia said.

"You're my best friend, Cha-Cha!" Robbie shouted.

"We're all in this together," Alexander slurred.

"I'll drink to that," Cha-Cha barked.

"Oh, Cha-Cha," Beth-Margaret laughed.

The family laughed and drank together. It was a good night.

CHARMING GUY

YOU THINK YOU'RE SO CHARMING?
SSSSS
CHARM THIS!
PHWEEE

I DON'T KNOW ABOUT THIS BEARD ANYMORE.
I THINK IT'S HANDSOME.
IT'S BECOME MY WHOLE IDENTITY.
YOU HAVE OTHER QUALITIES TOO.
LIKE...
...A MUSTACHE.
THAT'S PART OF THE BEARD.
SHIT

SMOKING DIDN'T MAKE
HIM COOL. THE HAWK
THAT WAS ALSO SMOKING
MADE HIM COOL.

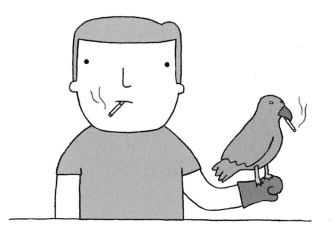

HEY, WE GOT A PACKAGE.
Bees
DO YOU THINK THERE'S BEES IN IT?
THAT SEEMS LIKE A REAL POSSIBILITY.
HERE.

THIS IS, LIKE, THE WORST GUN WE HAVE.
CAN YOU JUST BE GRATEFUL?
FUCKING HATE THIS GUN.
NUDGE

BZZZZ
Bees
POW
POW
POW
POW
POW
POW
POW
PEW
PEW
PEW
PEW
PEW
AH!

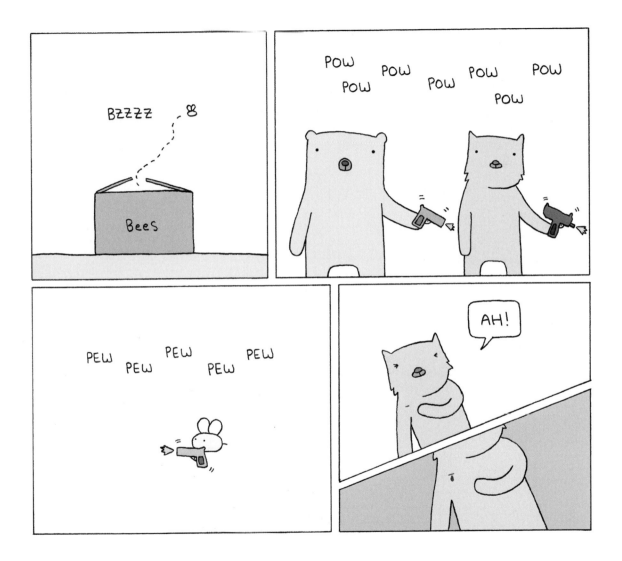

I'M GONNA DIE, I'M ALLERGIC.
BUT HE SHOT YOU WITH A GUN.
I'M ALLERGIC TO GUNS.
OH SHIT MAN.
MY LIFE FLASHES...
CHIPS

FUCK, I WAS AWESOME.
NOOOOOO OOOOOOO
OOOOOO OOOOO—
—AW HELL YEAH.
—OOOOOOO OOOOOOOoo

ACKNOWLEDGMENTS

Thank you, everyone who helped me make this book. Thank you, editor. Thank you, agent. Thank you, employees of coffee store. Thank you, supportive friends. Thank you, family. Thank you, David Bowie. Thank you, people who found my comics on the Internet and read them and helped make them popular. Thank you, sandwiches. Thank you, feverish nightmares. Thank you, sound of the wind gently rustling the trees outside my window. Thank you, '90s cartoons. Thank you, animals in human clothing. Thank you, headphones.

You're all cool.

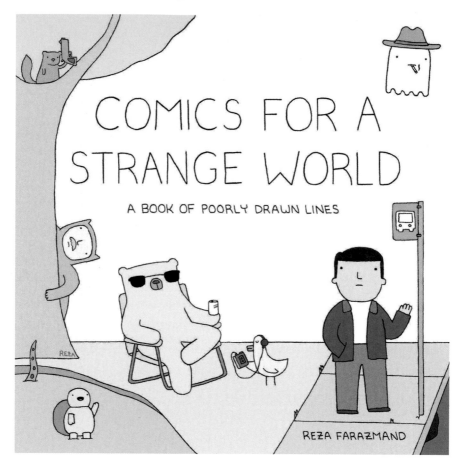

Also by Reza Farazmand

On sale October 24, 2017

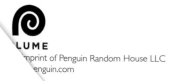

LUME
Imprint of Penguin Random House LLC
penguin.com